W9-AZG-432

Symbols of American Freedom

The Gettysburg Battlefield

by Ellen Todras

Series Consultant: Jerry D. Thompson,
Regents Professor of History,
Texas A&M International University

CHELSEA CLUBHOUSE

An Imprint of Chelsea House Publishers

Symbols of American Freedom: The Gettysburg Battlefield

Chelsea Clubhouse
An imprint of Chelsea House Publishers
132 West 31st Street
New York NY 10001

Library of Congress Cataloging-in-Publication Data
Todras, Ellen H., 1947-
      The Gettysburg battlefield / by Ellen Todras.
            p. cm. — (Symbols of American freedom)
      Includes index.
      ISBN 978-1-60413-514-5
      1. Gettysburg, Battle of, Gettysburg, Pa., 1863—Juvenile literature. 2. Gettysburg National Military Park (Pa.)—Juvenile literature. I. Title. II. Series.
      E475.53.T636 2010
      973.7'349—dc22   2009005734

Developed for Chelsea House by RJF Publishing LLC (www.RJFpublishing.com)
Text and cover design by Tammy West/Westgraphix LLC
Maps by Stefan Chabluk
Photo research by Edward A. Thomas
Index by Nila Glikin

Photo Credits: 5: Shutterstock; 6, 23: © Bettmann/Corbis; 9, 43: Getty Images; 11, 36: © North Wind Picture Archives/Photolibrary; 13: Library of Congress LC-USZ62-72765; 14: Library of Congress LC-DIG-cwpb-04402; 15: Collection of The New-York Historical Society, Image #ac03149; 16: Library of Congress LC-USZC2-1956; 17: Library of Congress LC-USZC4-3365; 19: Library of Congress LC-USZC4-1760; 20: United States Sanitary Commission records, Manuscripts and Archives Division, The New York Public Library, Astor, Lenox, and Tilden Foundations; 24: Library of Congress LC-USZ62-77370; 28: Library of Congress LC-DIG-cwpbh-03163; 29: USAMIL; 32: Library of Congress LC-DIG-cwpbh-03216; 33: © imac/Alamy; 35: © Corbis; 39: Library of Congress LC-DIG-hec-02890; 40, 41: Associated Press.

Note: Quotations in the text are used essentially as originally written. In some cases, spelling, punctuation, and the like have been modernized to aid student understanding.

Table of Contents

Words that are defined in the Glossary are in **bold** type
the first time they appear in the text.

Chapter 1

The Importance of Gettysburg

Gettysburg is a town in Pennsylvania. It is also a national military park. The park marks the site of the most important battle of the Civil War.

If you visit Gettysburg National Military Park today, you see rolling fields and hills covered with trees. Beautiful statues dot the landscape. It is hard to imagine that a three-day battle was fought here by over 150,000 men. But that is what happened on July 1–3, 1863, during the American Civil War.

The Civil War

A **civil war** is a war between people of the same country. The American Civil War took place between 1861 and 1865. It was also called the War Between the States.

The parts of the country that fought each other were the North and the South. The North and the South had very different ways of life. The most important difference between the two regions was slavery. Nearly 4 million African-American slaves lived in the South when the war began. The South had many large farms, called plantations. Landowners grew crops on the plantations. The most important crop in the South was cotton. Many hands were needed to work a cotton plantation. Landowners depended on slaves to do this back-breaking labor.

Unlike the South, the North did not have plantations. It had many cities where people worked in factories. The North also had a great many small family farms.

Another big difference separated the two regions. Many people in the South believed that if their state did not want to follow a national law, it did not have to. They thought that if the United States tried to force a state to follow its laws, the state could **secede**—or withdraw from the **Union**. (The Union

This statue at Gettysburg National Military Park honors General George Meade, who commanded the Union Army at the Battle of Gettysburg.

A slave family picks cotton on a plantation in Georgia before the Civil War.

was another name many people used at that time for the United States.) People who believed states had a right to secede were called **secessionists**.

These differences between the North and the South became more and more important during the 1800s. New states were settled and became part of the United States. Some states became free states (states that did not allow slavery). Other states became slave states. People in the South worried that there were going to be more free states than slave states. People in the North worried that slavery would spread across the entire continent of North America. The 1850s were a time of great unrest. More and more people came to believe that the North and the South would not be able to settle their differences peacefully.

The Election of 1860

The election of 1860 brought the serious differences between North and South to a head. Running as the Republican candidate for president was Abraham Lincoln. He was personally against slavery, and he did not want it to be allowed in new states. He also stood for keeping the Union together. He did not believe that states had a right to secede.

When the Democratic Party held its convention in April 1860 to choose a candidate for president, it split into two parties over the issue of slavery.

The Northern Democrats wanted new states to be able to choose whether to be slave or free. The Southern Democrats wanted slavery to be allowed everywhere in the United States.

A fourth party formed as well, the Constitutional Union Party. Its goal was to keep things as they were. It promised not to take a stand on the issues dividing North and South.

Eighty-one percent of voters went to the polls on November 6, 1860. When the votes were counted, Lincoln had won the most votes in enough states to get 180 votes in the Electoral College. This compared to 72 for the

Abraham Lincoln (1809–1865)

Abraham Lincoln was born in a log cabin in Kentucky in 1809. His family moved to Indiana when he was 7. In 1830, when he was 21, they moved to Illinois. There, he became a lawyer and politician. Lincoln was known for his common sense, honesty, and fairness.

When the Republican Party formed in 1854, Lincoln was a strong supporter in Illinois. He ran for the United States Senate in 1858. Running against him was Stephen A. Douglas. Lincoln and Douglas held debates about slavery across the state of Illinois. Lincoln believed that slavery should not be allowed in new states being added to the Union. Douglas believed that each new state should decide for itself whether to allow slavery. During the election campaign, Lincoln said:

> "A house divided against itself cannot stand. I believe this government cannot endure [last], permanently half slave and half free."

Lincoln lost the election to the Senate. Yet he gained national fame through his speeches about slavery. Two years later, he was elected president of the United States on the Republican Party ticket.

Lincoln led the Union throughout the long and difficult Civil War. He was re-elected to a second term as president in 1864. Then, on April 14, 1865, just as the war was ending, Lincoln was shot by John Wilkes Booth as the president watched a play in a Washington, D.C., theater. Lincoln died the next day.

The Electoral College

Officially, the president of the United States is chosen by the members (called electors) of the Electoral College. Each state has a number of electors equal to its number of senators and representatives in Congress. On Election Day, when people go to vote for their choice for president, the candidate who wins the most votes in a state wins that state's electors. The electors then meet after Election Day to formally choose the president.

Southern Democrats, 39 for the Constitutional Party, and 12 for the Northern Democrats. Abraham Lincoln would be the next president.

Most of Lincoln's votes had come from the North. Lincoln said he would not take any action against slavery in the states where it already existed. But many people in the South believed that their way of life was threatened by his election. Six weeks after the election, South Carolina became the first southern state to secede. Six more states soon followed—Mississippi, Florida, Alabama, Georgia, Louisiana, and Texas.

By the time Lincoln took office in March 1861, these seven states had formed the Confederate States of America. They believed that President Lincoln would free all the slaves. He tried to convince them he would not do this, but they did not listen.

On April 12, 1861, Confederate forces fired on Fort Sumter in Charleston Harbor in South Carolina. They captured the fort the next day. The Civil War had begun. In the next few weeks, four more southern states joined the Confederacy—Virginia, Arkansas, North Carolina, and Tennessee.

Strengths and Weaknesses

At the beginning of the war, each side had a simple goal. The states in the Union were fighting to keep the United States a single country. The

Confederate states wanted their independence. They no longer wanted to be part of the United States.

In this conflict, the Union had some very important advantages. First, it had 18 million people. The Confederacy had only about 9 million, and some 3.5 million of them were slaves. Nine out of every ten factories in the country were in the North. Also, the North had most of the country's iron, copper, and coal. It could make weapons and other war materials more easily. The North had more railroads and ships, as well. It could move armies and supplies more quickly than the South could. It could **blockade** southern ports and keep the South from trading with European countries for war materials and other things the South needed.

Abraham Lincoln (left in the picture above) and Stephen A. Douglas debate about slavery in 1858.

But the Confederates also had certain advantages. Most battles were fought on southern soil. So Confederate soldiers might fight harder because they were defending their own land. Many United States army officers came from the South. When the Confederacy was formed, these

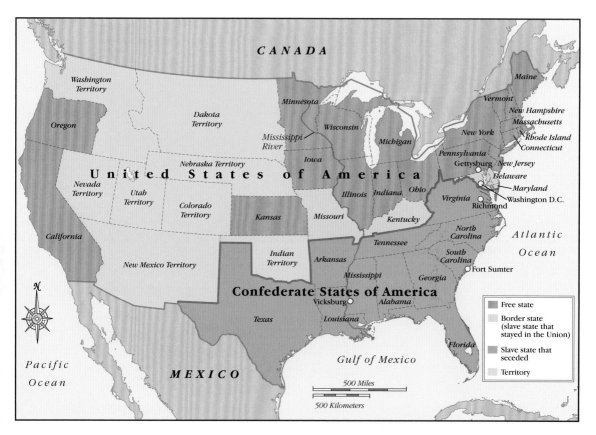

At the beginning of the Civil War, there were 11 slave states that had seceded and formed the Confederate States of America. Four slave states stayed in the Union.

Border States

When the Civil War began, there were 15 slave states. Eleven seceded and formed the Confederacy. The other four—Delaware, Maryland, Kentucky, and Missouri—stayed in the Union. These states became known as the border states. They were just over the border from the Confederacy. Many people in these states wanted the South to win, and some of them went to fight in Confederate armies. But many other people favored staying in the Union.

officers often sided with their home states. This meant that the Confederate armies had the benefit of many good generals and other officers.

Also, to win the war, all the Confederacy had to do was to not lose. In order to win, the North had to conquer the South and force the southern states to rejoin the Union. The South did not have to conquer anything. It just had to keep fighting and

The Confederate attack on Fort Sumter (above) in Charleston, South Carolina, was the first battle of the Civil War.

not be defeated. If it kept fighting long enough and enough people in the North grew tired of the war and its cost in lives and money, then the North might decide to stop the war and let the southern states go their own way.

Turning Point at Gettysburg

By the summer of 1863, many people in the North were indeed growing tired of the long and costly war. A victory for the Union forces at Gettysburg was all-important. If the Union Army lost, it might mean the end of the war.

That is why the Battle of Gettysburg was such an important turning point in the Civil War. After the North won, Gettysburg became a symbol of the union of the states into a single country—the United States. It also came to stand for the belief in "liberty for all" that is so important to Americans, then and now.

The Fate of the Country Hung in the Balance

When the Civil War began, people on both sides were filled with excitement. President Lincoln called for 75,000 men to serve in the army. Instead, hundreds of thousands volunteered. They came from every state remaining in the Union. (A few even came from southern states that had seceded.) Jane Stuart Woolsey, a young woman from New York, wrote in a letter to a friend in Paris, France: "It seems as if we were never alive till now, never had a country till now." Equally thrilled were most southerners in the Confederacy.

Both sides expected the war to last only a few months. Instead, it lasted for four long years. By the time it was over, almost 500,000 soldiers on both sides had died—more American deaths than in any other war in U.S. history. Confederate armies won many of the battles in the first two years. The Union had trouble finding generals who could make good decisions.

Union soldiers from New York stand guard near Harpers Ferry, Virginia, in 1861.

Civil War Armies

Huge armies fought the battles of the Civil War. There were three main kinds of forces fighting on land. The **infantry** included the soldiers (or troops) who fought on foot. The **artillery** was the part of an army that used cannons, large guns that were attached to frames with wheels. The **cavalry** included the soldiers who fought on horseback.

Armies were organized into units, or groups, of different sizes (see table). A platoon was a small unit. A company was a larger unit that had several platoons in it. A battalion had several companies in it, and so on. Each type of unit was usually led by an officer of a certain rank.

Organization of Civil War Armies

Name of Unit	Number of Soldiers	Officer Who Commanded
platoon	20 – 50 troops	Lieutenant
company	100 – 250 troops	Captain or major
battalion	400 – 1,200 troops	Lieutenant colonel
brigade or regiment	2,000 – 8,000 troops	Colonel or brigadier general
division	7,000 – 22,000 troops	Lieutenant general
corps	50,000 or more troops	General

The war was fought on several different **fronts**, or parts of the country. The campaign in the West focused on control of the Mississippi River. The naval campaign focused on control of the waters near the coast, both in the Atlantic Ocean and in the Gulf of Mexico. The largest campaign was fought on land in the East, near the mid-Atlantic **seaboard**. Many of the battles in the East took place in Virginia, where the Confederate capital of Richmond was located. Virginia was also just across the Potomac River

Robert E. Lee (1807–1870)

Robert Edward Lee was born in Virginia in 1807. He was the son of a Revolutionary War hero. He married the great-granddaughter of George Washington's wife. So he was well aware of Americans' efforts to form the new country of the United States. Lee graduated from the United States Military Academy at West Point, second in his class. He fought well in the Mexican-American War in the 1840s. When Virginia seceded, Lee felt that he had to support his state. "I cannot raise my hand against my birthplace, my home, my children," he wrote.

Lee's plantation at Arlington, Virginia, just outside Washington, D.C., was taken over by Union forces. In 1864, it became the site of Arlington National Cemetery, where soldiers and former soldiers are buried. After the Civil War, Lee became president of Washington College (later Washington and Lee University) in Lexington, Virginia.

With flags flying and bands playing, Union soldiers march off to join the Civil War. This picture is a large poster made from smaller pieces put together.

from Washington, D.C., the Union capital. The presence of large enemy armies in Virginia presented a threat to both capitals.

The Army of Northern Virginia Finds a Leader

For the Confederates, the Army of Northern Virginia fought most of the large battles in the East, usually on Virginia's soil. In charge of this army was a deeply beloved and respected—and a highly skilled—general, Robert E. Lee.

15

Posters like this one urged men to volunteer to join the army.
At the beginning of the war, President Lincoln asked for 75,000
volunteers—and got hundreds of thousands.

Lee became the commander of the Army of Northern Virginia in 1862. He reorganized the army, improving discipline and raising **morale**. Morale means the mood or spirit of the troops. Because the Union Army was always larger than the Confederate forces, Lee tried to gain the advantage by attacking first and surprising the enemy.

From Fredericksburg to Gettysburg

A high point of the war for the Confederacy came in late 1862 and early 1863. The Battle of Fredericksburg took place in December 1862 in Fredericksburg,

Union soldiers on the attack at the Battle of Fredericksburg. The Confederate forces had the high ground and beat back the attack. About 13,000 Union soldiers were killed or wounded in the battle.

Virginia. The Union Army in Virginia was called the Army of the Potomac. General Lee outsmarted the Union general by stationing his army on higher ground. The Union forces tried to attack, but the attack was a complete failure. A total of 13,000 Union soldiers were killed or wounded in the battle, compared to 5,000 **casualties** for the Army of Northern Virginia.

Next, the two armies met at Chancellorsville, Virginia, in May 1863. President Lincoln had appointed a new general, "Fighting Joe" Hooker, to lead the Army of the Potomac. Hooker had twice as many troops as Lee. Lee surprised Hooker, however. He sent Stonewall Jackson, his best general, to attack the Union Army's right side. Once again, the Union forces were defeated. Among the Confederate wounded, however, was General Jackson. He died a few days later.

During the battles, President Lincoln would go to the telegraph office in Washington several times a day. When Lincoln got the news about the defeat at Chancellorsville, his face turned white. "My God! My God! What will the country say?" a newspaperman heard him cry out.

The Confederates, on the other hand, celebrated. They hoped that the war would soon be over. They believed that General Lee and his troops could beat the Union forces anytime they fought.

A Bold Plan

After Chancellorsville, General Lee returned to Richmond. He reported to the president of the Confederacy, Jefferson Davis, and Davis's staff. Lee wanted to invade Pennsylvania, a northern state. He believed his army could beat the Union Army on its own soil. This would further lower morale in the North and possibly make many more northerners want to simply stop fighting the war. Lee could also feed his troops from the rich Pennsylvania farmlands and get other supplies for his army. In addition, the South was trying to get Great Britain and other countries to recognize

The Confederates won the Battle of Chancellorsville, but General Stonewall Jackson (second from right) was seriously wounded and died soon after.

the Confederate States of America as a new country and to send weapons and other supplies to the South to help it fight the war. A victory by Lee in Pennsylvania would make Great Britain and France more likely to help the South. For all of these reasons, Davis agreed to Lee's bold plan.

Changes in the Army of the Potomac

After Chancellorsville, the Union forces pulled back. Morale was low in the Army of the Potomac. Many of the troops had lost faith in General Hooker's leadership. When the Union Army commanders figured out that Lee was headed north, they followed. The Union Army was farther east than Lee's and traveling about a day behind.

The Union troops were not the only ones who had lost faith in General Hooker. President Lincoln was convinced that Hooker was afraid to fight

Gettysburg was a small quiet town in 1863 on the eve of the battle.

General Lee again. On June 28, he made General George Meade the commander of the Army of the Potomac. Meade had been leading one corps of troops within the Army of the Potomac. It was a huge task to take control of an enormous army—about 90,000 troops in all—just days before a great battle.

As the Union Army crossed into Pennsylvania, **civilians** lined the roads and cheered them in their march north. Civilians are people who are not soldiers. The soldiers' spirits lifted. The troops were also determined to defend northern soil.

In Their Own Words

A Boost for Morale

Surgeon Edwin Hutchinson was a doctor in the Union Army. In a letter to his mother on July 1, 1863, he wrote:

"Our men are three times as enthusiastic as they have been in Virginia. The idea that Pennsylvania is invaded and that we are fighting on our own soil proper influences them strongly. They are more determined than I have ever before seen them."

Civilians in Pennsylvania were worried about the Confederates being in their region. They gave them food and other goods when the Confederates demanded it. Civilians also grew concerned when it became clear that both armies were nearby. Would a battle be fought on their land? Would their homes and property be destroyed?

On June 30, Confederate General A. P. Hill heard of a supply of shoes in the town of Gettysburg. He ordered a division of men to go there and get the shoes. But the Confederates saw that some Union cavalry was in the town. The Confederates did not enter Gettysburg or engage in battle. They reported back that the enemy was nearby. General Lee began to gather his forces to the west of Gettysburg, on Seminary Ridge. (A ridge is a line of hills or high ground.)

The Union cavalry was commanded by General John Buford. He had noted that many roads ran through Gettysburg. He also saw that the town was set between two rows of hills. An army on a hill would have an advantage over an enemy having to climb the hill to attack. Gettysburg would be a good place for a battle.

3

A Downpour
of Bullets

As July 1, 1863, dawned in Gettysburg, thousands of troops were on the march in the surrounding countryside. Confederate troops were heading southeast toward Seminary Ridge. Union troops were marching west and north. General Meade had ordered most of his troops to start marching toward Gettysburg. Each army was heading straight toward the enemy—but did not yet know exactly where most of the enemy forces were.

The Battle: Day 1

The battle began a few hours later. Confederate troops met a small force of Union soldiers outside of town. Although outnumbered three-to-one, the Union troops held off the Confederates for several hours. In the meantime, troops from both sides rushed to the sound of battle. As the Union troops tired, **reinforcements** came in and took their places. Reinforcements are new troops entering a battle. The Union line held. By mid-afternoon about 24,000

Confederates were battling 19,000 Union soldiers. The line of battle looked like a semicircle to the west of Gettysburg.

Late in the day, Confederate divisions attacked from the north. The Union forces retreated from the town of Gettysburg. The Confederates took control of it. More Union troops arrived and held the line south of the town. They positioned themselves on Culp's Hill, on Cemetery Hill, and on Cemetery Ridge. The Union line extended for several miles, ending on the left at a hill called Little Round Top.

Fierce fighting involving tens of thousands of troops went on for three days at the Battle of Gettysburg.

General Longstreet (on horseback in the center of the picture above) did not think the Confederates should attack the Union position at Gettysburg.

Across the way, on Seminary Ridge, Lee and one of the generals in his army, James Longstreet, were also thinking about the position of the enemy troops. Lee had a total of about 75,000 soldiers in his Army of Northern Virginia, compared to Meade's 90,000 men. Many thought Longstreet was Lee's best general, now that Stonewall Jackson had been killed. Longstreet did not think that attacking the Union Army position could succeed. Lee disagreed.

The Battle: Day 2

General Lee's plan for July 2 had two parts. General Longstreet would attack the Union Army on its left, along Cemetery Ridge. Lee expected the Union Army to move troops from its center to defend this attack. Then, Lee would send another force to attack on the right, on Culp's Hill and Cemetery Hill. Lee thought the Union forces would not hold up against a two-pronged attack—and the Confederates would win.

Local People on the Battlefront

For some people living in Gettysburg, like teenager Daniel Skelly, having a battle in one's town was a thrill. On July 1, Daniel climbed a tree so he could see the fighting on the ridge to the west. He stayed there until **shells** began falling around him. A shell is a hollow metal object full of explosives that is fired from a cannon.

Adults were more worried about the town and their loved ones. Sarah Broadhead was in her kitchen when the artillery started firing on July 1. "People were running here and there, screaming that the town would be shelled," she later wrote. "No one knew where to go or what to do."

Those with the most to fear were free African Americans who lived in or near Gettysburg. If captured by the Confederates, they could be shot or taken into slavery. Many hid or went farther north until the danger was over.

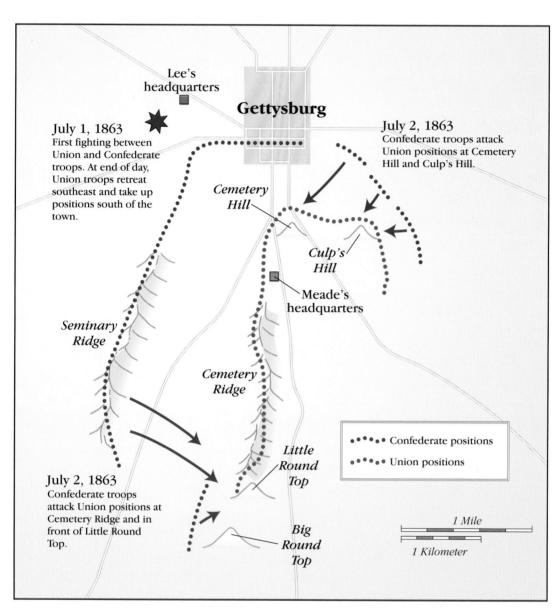

Lee's headquarters

Gettysburg

July 1, 1863
First fighting between Union and Confederate troops. At end of day, Union troops retreat southeast and take up positions south of the town.

July 2, 1863
Confederate troops attack Union positions at Cemetery Hill and Culp's Hill.

Cemetery Hill

Culp's Hill

Meade's headquarters

Seminary Ridge

Cemetery Ridge

July 2, 1863
Confederate troops attack Union positions at Cemetery Ridge and in front of Little Round Top.

Little Round Top

Big Round Top

• • • • • Confederate positions
• • • • • Union positions

1 Mile

1 Kilometer

On the first day of battle, Union and Confederate forces fought west of Gettysburg and then took up positions south of the town. Two attacks by the Confederates on July 2 were beaten back by Union troops.

In Their Own Words

Lee's Decision

General Longstreet believed that the Union Army's position was too strong and that Lee should not fight the Army of the Potomac at Gettysburg. But Lee thought he could win and was determined to attack. Pointing toward Cemetery Hill, he said to Longstreet:

"The enemy is there, and I am going to attack him there."

Lee wanted Longstreet to launch his attack as quickly as possible. But Longstreet rested his troops in the morning, since they had marched during the night to reach Gettysburg. Then, General Lee's guide took them on a roundabout route to the place from which they would start their attack. This was to avoid being seen by Union forces. As a result, Longstreet did not attack until the late afternoon. This allowed the Union forces to rest and to prepare for the attack. When Longstreet finally sent his forces across the open land between the ridges, he saw to his surprise that part of the Union Army had moved forward. General Dan Sickles had moved his Third Corps about a mile closer to the Confederates. This move had several results. The Confederates could attack this corps on two sides, and the Third Corps was destroyed that day. General Sickles was wounded and lost his leg that day, too.

The move also left Little Round Top undefended. Union General Gouverneur Warren, chief of engineers, noticed this just as the Confederates were moving to take the hill. (His job was to identify positions that were good places to stage a battle.) Warren saw that if the Confederates got Little Round Top, they could crush the left end of the Union Army.

In Their Own Words

Defending Little Round Top

One of the Union units fighting on Little Round Top was the 20th Maine. Colonel Joshua L. Chamberlain (right) led this regiment. A year earlier Chamberlain had been a college professor. He took a leave of absence and joined the Union Army.

That day on Little Round Top, smoke and fire filled the air. Men were surrounded by the whistle of bullets and the groans of dying men. Chamberlain later wrote:

> "The two lines [Union and Confederate] met and broke and intermingled in the shock. The crush of [rifles] gave way to cuts and thrusts, grapplings and wrestlings. The edge of conflict swayed to and fro…. At times I saw around me more of the enemy than of my own men; gaps opening, swallowing, closing again with sharp…energy."

With each attack, men from both sides were mowed down. Yet the Alabama soldiers kept coming back. Chamberlain saw that his men were running out of **ammunition**, or bullets. He commanded them to fix their **bayonets**, or long knives, at the ends of their rifles. Then he and his men charged down the hill, yelling as if their lives depended on it. They broke the line of Alabamans. Little Round Top was saved.

Warren rode quickly to the commander of the Fifth Corps, General George Sykes. Sykes sent Union troops hurrying up Little Round Top. They got there just in time to defend it. A brigade of Confederates from Alabama was already climbing the hill. For the next few hours, some of the worst fighting of the day took place on Little Round Top. At the end of the bloody fighting, the Union troops had held the hill.

The Confederate attack on the Union's right side was supposed to happen around the same time as Longstreet's attack. However, it did not start until Longstreet's attack was ending. The Confederates almost gained Culp's Hill and Cemetery Hill. They were pushed down again after sunset.

At the day's end on July 2, both forces were in much the same position as they had been when the day started. The Union's Third Corps had been pushed back, but these men had been out of position. The loss of that land did not threaten the Union's line. The question in everyone's mind was: Would the Confederates try to attack again?

Union soldiers of the 20th Maine regiment fight to hold Little Round Top on July 2.

Chapter 4

The Union Holds

The leaders of both the Union and the Confederate armies held midnight councils to plan out the next day of battle—and to decide whether they would fight on a third day. General Lee still believed his troops could win. He decided to hit the Union line in its center. There, he thought, it was weakest. General Longstreet would again command the attack. Lee also would send a cavalry division to attack the Union Army from the rear. Another corps would hit the Union line on its right side.

General Meade correctly believed that the Confederates would attack the Union Army at its center. He told his men to prepare for that. Then, the Army of the Potomac waited to see whether Meade was right.

The Battle: Day 3

At first, Meade appeared to be wrong. At daybreak, fighting broke out on the right at Culp's

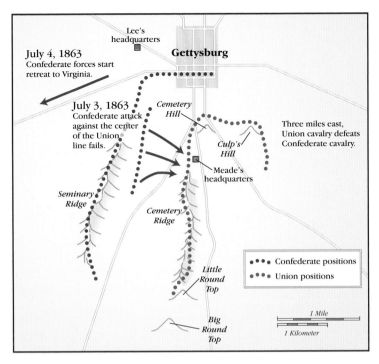

On July 3, the major fighting took place when the Confederates launched a large-scale attack against the center of the Union line. When that attack failed, the Union Army had won the Battle of Gettysburg.

Hill. After seven hours, the Union troops regained land they had lost the day before.

Lee was still determined to go ahead with his attack on the Union center. He ordered a mighty artillery attack before his infantry charged. He gathered 150 cannons in the largest Confederate bombardment of the war. Around 1 o'clock in the afternoon, he launched this attack. For two hours Union and Confederate artillery battered each other. The roar was so loud, it was heard in the city of Pittsburgh. That was more than 150 miles (240 kilometers) away.

Finally, the Union guns grew silent. Longstreet ordered three divisions, led by Generals George Pickett and A. P. Hill, to attack. They led 15,000 men across three-quarters of a mile (1¼ kilometers) of open land. The attack became known as Pickett's Charge. It was doomed to failure. The Union artillery chief had silenced his guns to make the Confederates think

Custer at Gettysburg

One of the Union officers who played a key role in defeating the Confederate cavalry attack on July 3 was 23-year-old brigadier general George Armstrong Custer. Custer had graduated at the bottom of his West Point class in 1861. Yet he distinguished himself in combat as a cavalry officer during the Civil War.

At Gettysburg, Custer did not wait for the approaching Confederate cavalry to attack. Instead, he cried out to his men to follow him. The opposing forces hit each other head-on. Horses reared up, crushing their own riders. In the end, the Union cavalry beat back the Confederates and kept them from attacking the Union infantry.

Less than 13 years later, Custer commanded several hundred cavalry troops in Montana Territory during the Indian Wars. He was trying to get bands (or groups) of Sioux to move onto reservations. Custer was supposed to wait for a second force of troops to join his. Instead, on June 25, 1876, he attacked a large Native American encampment on the Little Bighorn River. This famous attack is often called Custer's Last Stand. Thousands of Native American warriors, led by Crazy Horse and other chiefs, killed Custer and more than 200 of his men at the Battle of the Little Bighorn.

he was out of ammunition. Instead, he waited for the Confederates to be within firing range. He then gave the order to fire.

Under this all-out assault, the Confederate attack stalled. Two or three hundred men led by General Lewis Armistead made it past the first Union line. This is called the High Water Mark of the Confederacy. It marks the point at which the Confederate Army was closest to victory. But the Confederates were beaten back. Armistead was wounded, and he died two days later. Only half of the men who set out across that open field returned. The whole charge took less than an hour.

The Confederate cavalry attack also was unsuccessful. All of Lee's efforts on July 3 had failed.

The next day was July 4, Independence Day. The Army of the Potomac had beaten the Confederates in a great battle. General Lee and his army began to move south again, in defeat.

The Cost of Battle

The human price of the Union victory at Gettysburg was high. Over 23,000 Union soldiers were dead, wounded, or missing. This was one-fourth of

This statue at Gettysburg National Military Park shows General Lewis Armistead lying seriously wounded after the failed Confederate attack on July 3.

In Their Own Words

Cornelia Hancock, Civil War Nurse

One woman who served as a nurse at Gettysburg was 23-year-old Cornelia Hancock. She came from a small village in New Jersey. Her sister's husband was a doctor in Philadelphia. When they heard about the battle in Gettysburg, he asked Cornelia to join him in caring for the wounded. They arrived in Gettysburg three days after the battle ended. Cornelia later wrote:

> "We went the same evening to one of the churches, where I saw for the first time what war meant. Hundreds of desperately wounded men were stretched out on boards laid across the high-backed pews as closely as they could be packed together. The boards were covered with straw. Thus [raised], these poor sufferers' faces, white and drawn with pain, were almost on a level with my own. I seemed to stand breast-high in a sea of [pain]."

Hancock stayed on as a volunteer nurse with the Union Army for two more years, until the war ended. Then she moved to South Carolina for 10 years. There she helped set up a school for freed slaves.

all the troops in the Army of the Potomac. The Confederate cost was even higher. There were 28,000 Confederate casualties—more than one-third of the troops in the Army of Northern Virginia.

A heavy rain fell on July 4. Horse-and-carriage ambulances and farm wagons began to carry the thousands of wounded men off the battlefield. These included 7,000 Confederate wounded, left behind for the Union doctors to care for.

The wounded were packed into homes, churches, and barns across Adams County, where Gettysburg was located. Some were left out in the mud under trees. There was not enough shelter for everyone.

Doctors and nurses from all over the North came to tend the wounded. Thousands of soldiers had to have an arm or leg amputated. Camp Letterman, a central hospital, was set up on July 22. It was made up of 2,400 tents. Each tent had 12 beds. Most nurses at that time were men. Yet many women volunteered as nurses too.

As the wounded began to get decent care, people's attention turned to the many thousands of dead on the battlefield. Many could not be sent home. Some had no identification on them. The people of Adams County asked the Pennsylvania legislature for help. It set aside funds to establish a Soldiers' National Cemetery for the Union dead at Gettysburg.

The cemetery was **dedicated** on November 19, 1863. A famous speaker, Edward Everett, talked for two hours. Then, President Lincoln gave a short

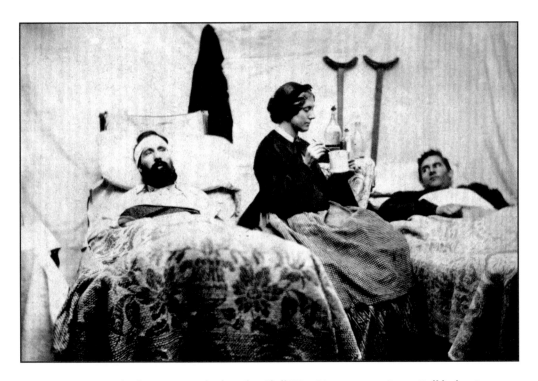

Many women worked as nurses during the Civil War. Here, nurse Anne Bell helps two wounded Union soldiers.

speech. His words became known as the Gettysburg Address (**address** can be another word for a speech). Lincoln's address gave a new focus to the war effort. It said that the North was fighting for freedom and democracy.

Beginning of the End

On July 4, 1863, a day after the Battle of Gettysburg ended, Confederate forces in Vicksburg, Mississippi, surrendered to Union forces. This gave the Union complete control of the Mississippi River. It cut off Texas, Louisiana, and Arkansas from the rest of the Confederacy. "This was the most Glorious Fourth I ever spent," one Ohio soldier wrote.

In Their Own Words

The Gettysburg Address

Abraham Lincoln's Gettysburg Address has become one of the most famous speeches ever given. Using very few words, it states important ideas in clear and beautiful language. The speech ends with these words:

> "We here highly resolve that these dead shall not have died in vain—that this nation, under God, shall have a new birth of freedom—and that government of the people, by the people, for the people, shall not perish from the earth."

Abraham Lincoln delivering the Gettysburg Address on November 19, 1863.

Ending Slavery

At the beginning of the Civil War, the North was fighting to restore the Union. President Lincoln had said he would not take any action against slavery in the South. But as the war dragged on and so many Union soldiers lost their lives, Lincoln changed his mind. He decided that the war should have a larger goal. On January 1, 1863, he issued a document called the Emancipation Proclamation. This document said that slaves in areas that were rebelling against the United States were now free. In December 1865, soon after the Civil War ended, the U.S. Constitution was changed. The Thirteenth Amendment made slavery illegal in all parts of the United States.

The defeats at Gettysburg and Vicksburg were the beginning of the end for the Confederacy. Yet the war went on for almost two more years. The Army of Northern Virginia never regained its former strength after Gettysburg. But Lee led the army safely back to Virginia, and it fought in many more battles over the next 21 months.

President Lincoln and others thought that General Meade should have chased and attacked Lee's army as it retreated from Gettysburg—and tried to destroy it. But Meade moved slowly and failed to cut off Lee's route back to Virginia.

General Ulysses S. Grant commanded the Union forces at Vicksburg. He also won other victories in the West. Lincoln believed Grant was a general who was not afraid to fight. In early 1864, he put Grant in charge of all the Union armies. Under Grant, the Army of the Potomac attacked Lee's army again and again. Finally, on April 9, 1865, Lee surrendered to Grant at Appomattox Courthouse, Virginia. Other Confederate armies surrendered soon after. The Civil War was over, the Union had been saved, and as a result of the war slavery became illegal in the entire United States.

Visiting Gettysburg Today

In 1864, citizens of Adams County, Pennsylvania, founded the Gettysburg Battlefield Memorial Association. Its purpose was to preserve parts of the battlefield as a **memorial** to Union troops that fought there. In 1895, the land was transferred to the United States government. Gettysburg National Military Park was formed. It was to be a memorial to the two armies that fought the largest battle of the Civil War. The U.S. National Park Service protects and preserves the site of the Battle of Gettysburg today.

The Great Reunion of 1913

As the 50-year anniversary of the Battle of Gettysburg drew near, the people of Pennsylvania decided to stage a reunion for all the soldiers who had fought there. Over 50,000 **veterans** came to Gettysburg that July of 1913. Former enemies walked the battlefield together, remembering the long-ago battle.

Former Union and Confederate soldiers march side by side at the 1913 reunion on the 50th anniversary of the Battle of Gettysburg.

The Gettysburg Cyclorama

In 1884 the French artist Paul Dominique Philippoteaux painted a cyclorama of the Battle of Gettysburg. A cyclorama is a huge painting with life-size figures. In front of the painting are objects that make viewers feel as if they are right there at the battle. Philippoteaux's cyclorama was of Pickett's Charge. Philippoteaux wanted to make the scene accurate. He hired photographers to make a series of pictures for his use. He also talked to veterans of the battle. The result is a 377-foot (115-meter) painting of Pickett's Charge. The cyclorama is housed today at Gettysburg National Military Park, where a major effort to **restore** it to its original glory began in 2003. The painting went on display again, in a new Visitor Center, in 2008.

One such man was A. C. Smith of the 56th Virginia Company. Crossing the land where Pickett's Charge took place, Smith told his fellow Confederates how he was wounded there. "I was shot right here where I stand now," he recalled. "I would have died if it hadn't been for a Union soldier, who saved my life. I've often wished I could see him, but I never saw him after that day."

Albert Hamilton, a Union veteran, was standing nearby. He overheard Smith and turned around and said, "That's...funny.... There was a Rebel here who was pretty badly hurt. I...took him upon my back and carried him...to the field hospital."

Smith grabbed Hamilton by the shoulder and looked at him for a long time. "You are the man!" he cried. They checked the records, and indeed, Hamilton had saved Smith's life by bringing him to the field hospital.

A highlight of the reunion was a reenactment of Pickett's Charge—the last major Confederate attack on July 3, 1863. The Union line waited as the Confederates walked slowly across the field. Instead of shooting as they met, however, the men shook hands.

For many people who go to Gettysburg today, viewing the large cyclorama painting of Pickett's Charge is a highlight of the visit.

In Their Own Words

Burying the Past

Bennet H. Young was the leader of an organization called the United Confederate Veterans. He came to the 1913 Great Reunion, where he was one of the people who spoke to the former soldiers. In his speech, he talked about Americans again being united as one people. He said:

"We are here, we of the South, and we are Americans; and we are here to tell the North so and to shake hands and let the dead past bury its dead. We are alive and we are all brothers, of a common blood and we fight for our country and die for it gladly. This is the South's message to the North."

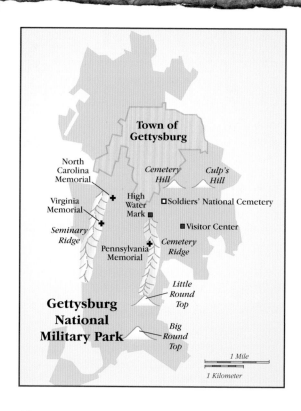

Gettysburg Today

People come to Gettysburg each year to re-enact the battle. They relive history as they wear Civil War uniforms and carry Civil War weapons. They join with others in acting out the different events of the battle.

Every year, more than 2 million other people also visit Gettysburg

People walking the battlefield today can see where the fiercest fighting took place, and they can view memorials to soldiers from various states, North and South, who lost their lives at Gettysburg in July 1863.

Visitors at Gettysburg National Military Park watch re-enactors (that is, people dressed as Civil War soldiers) re-create part of the famous battle.

National Military Park. They walk the battlefield and note the **monuments** built to honor the different heroes or troops who fought there. There are 1,328 monuments at Gettysburg. This is the largest collection of outdoor sculpture in the world.

Before July 1, 1863, Gettysburg was a quiet American town like thousands of others across the United States. The events of the Battle of Gettysburg and the deaths of so many men there have given Gettysburg a special place in American history. Gettysburg stands for the sacrifice so many soldiers made for their belief in their country and in freedom.

Timeline ★ ★ ★ ★ ★ ★ ★ ★ ★

★ **1854**   The Republican Party is formed.

★ **1858**   Abraham Lincoln and Stephen A. Douglas hold a series of debates in Illinois and disagree about slavery.

★ **1860**   Republican candidate Abraham Lincoln is elected president. South Carolina secedes from Union.

★ **1861**   The Confederate States of America is formed. By June it includes a total of 11 southern states that have seceded. **April:** Fort Sumter is fired on; the Civil War begins.

★ **1862**   General Robert E. Lee's Confederate forces win the Battle of Fredericksburg.

★ **1863**   **January 1:** President Lincoln issues the Emancipation Proclamation. This document declares that slaves in areas of the Confederacy still rebelling against the United States are now free. **May:** Lee's army wins the Battle of Chancellorsville. **July 1-3:** The Union Army defeats Lee's army at the Battle of Gettysburg. **July 4:** A Union Army led by General Ulysses S. Grant captures Vicksburg, giving the Union control of the entire Mississippi River. **November 19:** The Soldiers' National Cemetery is dedicated at Gettysburg; Lincoln delivers the Gettysburg Address.

★ **1864**   The Gettysburg Battlefield Memorial Association is formed to preserve the site of the battle. Lincoln is re-elected to a second term as president.

★ **1865**   Lee surrenders to Grant; the Civil War ends in a Union victory. President Lincoln is assassinated. The Thirteenth Amendment to the U.S. Constitution officially ends slavery in the United States.

★ **1895**   The Gettysburg Battlefield Memorial Association gives the land it was protecting to the U.S. government, and Gettysburg National Military Park is formed.

★ **1913**   Former soldiers gather for a reunion at Gettysburg on the 50th anniversary of the battle.

address: A speech.

ammunition: Bullets.

artillery: The part of an army that uses large, mounted guns, or cannons; also the guns themselves.

bayonet: A long knife at the end of a rifle.

blockade: To set up a barrier, such as a line of ships outside a port, to keep goods and people from getting in or out.

casualties: The number of soldiers killed or wounded.

cavalry: Soldiers who fight on horseback.

civil war: A war between people of the same country.

civilians: People who are not soldiers.

dedicate: To mark the opening of.

front: An area where fighting is going on.

infantry: Soldiers who fight on foot.

memorial: A landmark or other place set aside because of its historic importance.

monument: Something built in honor of a person or event.

morale: Mood or spirit.

reinforcements: New troops entering a battle.

restore: To put something back to its original conditions, such as by cleaning or repairing it.

seaboard: Land that is near the coast of an ocean or sea.

secede: To withdraw from, or leave, such as a state leaving the Union.

secessionists: People who believed, before the Civil War, that their state had a right to secede.

shell: A hollow metal object full of explosives that is fired from a cannon.

Union: Another name for the United States.

veteran: A former member of the armed forces.

To Learn More ★ ★ ★ ★ ★ ★ ★

Read these books

Abnett, Dan. *The Battle of Gettysburg: Spilled Blood on Sacred Ground*. New York: Rosen Publishing, 2006.

Burgan, Michael. *The Battle of Gettysburg*. Minneapolis: Compass Point, 2001.

Ford, Carin T. *The Battle of Gettysburg and Lincoln's Gettysburg Address*. Berkeley Heights, N.J.: Enslow Publishers, 2004.

Fradin, Dennis B. *The Battle of Gettysburg*. New York: Marshall Cavendish Benchmark, 2008.

Hale, Sarah Elder, ed. *Gettysburg: Bold Battle in the North*. Peterborough, N.H.: Cobblestone, 2005.

Hopkinson, Deborah. *Billy and the Rebel: Based on a True Civil War Story*. New York: Atheneum Books for Young Readers, 2005.

January, Brendan. *Gettysburg, July 1-3, 1863*. New York: Enchanted Lion Books, 2004.

King, David C. *The Battle of Gettysburg*. Woodbridge, Conn.: Blackbirch Press, 2001.

Stanchak, John. *Civil War* (Eyewitness Books). New York: Dorling Kindersley, 2000.

Look up these Web sites

Gettysburg National Military Park official Web site:
http://www.nps.gov/gett/index.htm

Gettysburg Battle Information and Living History Events:
http://www.gettysburg.com/livinghistory/index.html

Key Internet search terms
Civil War, Gettysburg, Robert E. Lee, Abraham Lincoln

The abbreviation *ill.* stands for illustration, and *ills.* stands for illustrations. Page references to illustrations and maps are in *italic* type.

Index ★ ★ ★ ★ ★ ★ ★ ★ ★

About the Author

Ellen Todras is a freelance writer and editor. She is the author of *Angelina Grimké: Voice of Abolition*, a young-adult biography. Todras has written parts of many social studies textbooks. She loves history, especially women's history and the Civil War. She lives in Eugene, Oregon.